PROTEST!
March for CHANGE

2018
MARCH for
OUR LIVES

by Joyce Markovics

CHERRY LAKE PRESS

Published in the United States of America by Cherry Lake Publishing Group
Ann Arbor, Michigan
www.cherrylakepublishing.com

Reading Adviser: Marla Conn, MS Ed., Literacy specialist, Read-Ability, Inc.
Content Adviser: Emilye Crosby, PhD
Book Designer: Ed Morgan

Photo Credits: © Zakari Kostzer/Shutterstock, cover and title page; Wikimedia Commons, 4; Wikimedia Commons, 5; © Joseph Gruber/Shutterstock, 6–7; © photo-denver/Shutterstock, 8; Wikimedia Commons, 9; Wikimedia Commons, 10; © Dave Collins/Associated Press, 11 left; Wikimedia Commons, 11 right; © Nicole Glass Photography/Shutterstock, 12; © damann/Shutterstock, 13; Wikimedia Commons, 14; Wikimedia Commons, 15; © Steven Senne/Associated Press, 16; Wikimedia Commons, 17; Andrew Harnik/Associated Press, 18; © Hayk_Shalunts/Shutterstock, 19; © Mark Dozier/Shutterstock, 20–21; © Jeff Pinette/Shutterstock, 21.

Cherry Lake Press is an imprint of Cherry Lake Publishing Group.

Library of Congress Cataloging-in-Publication Data
Names: Markovics, Joyce L., author.
Title: 2018 March for Our Lives / by Joyce Markovics.
Description: Ann Arbor, Michigan : Cherry Lake Publishing, 2021. | Series:
   Protest! March for change series | Includes bibliographical references
   and index. | Audience: Grades 2-3
Identifiers: LCCN 2020039587 (print) | LCCN 2020039588 (ebook) | ISBN
   9781534186347 (Hardcover) | ISBN 9781534186422 (Paperback) | ISBN
   9781534186507 (PDF) | ISBN 9781534186583 (eBook)
Subjects: LCSH: March for Our Lives (2018 : Washington, D.C.)—Juvenile
   literature. | Parkland Shooting, Parkland, Fla., 2018—Juvenile
   literature | School shootings—United States—Juvenile literature. |
   Student movements—United States—Juvenile literature.. | Political
   activists—Florida—Parkland—Juvenile literature. |
   Teenagers—Political activity—United States—Juvenile literature. | Gun
   control—United States—Juvenile literature. | National Rifle
   Association of America—Juvenile literature. | Marjory Stoneman Douglas
   High School (Parkland, Fla.)—Juvenile literature.
Classification: LCC LB3013.33.F6 M38 2021 (print) | LCC LB3013.33.F6
   (ebook) | DDC 371.7/820973—dc23
LC record available at https://lccn.loc.gov/2020039587
LC ebook record available at https://lccn.loc.gov/2020039588

Printed in the United States of America
Corporate Graphics

CONTENTS

ENOUGH IS ENOUGH

High school student Emma González looked into a crowd of 800,000 faces in Washington, D.C. It was March 24, 2018. She read the names of the 17 **victims** of the shooting at her high school in Parkland, Florida, a month earlier. As she did, tears streamed down her face. Then González stood silent for several minutes.

Emma González

"Since the time I came out here, it has been 6 minutes and 20 seconds," she said. That's how long it took for a gunman to kill 14 students and 3 staff at Marjory Stoneman Douglas High School on February 14, 2018. González survived the attack.

"Fight for your lives before it is someone else's job," González said at the end of her speech. Many of the marchers cheered. Some also wept. Few would forget her powerful message that day.

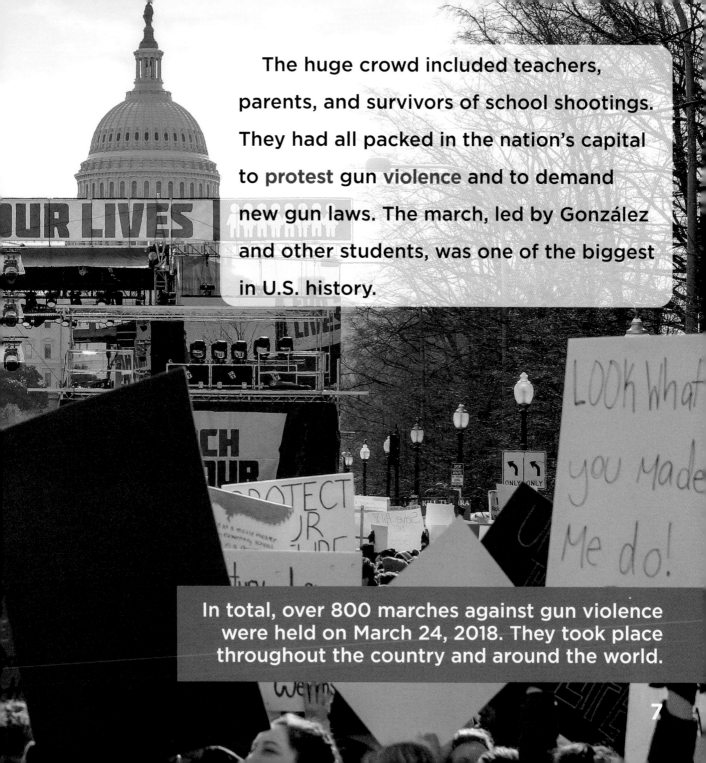

The huge crowd included teachers, parents, and survivors of school shootings. They had all packed in the nation's capital to **protest** gun **violence** and to demand new gun laws. The march, led by González and other students, was one of the biggest in U.S. history.

In total, over 800 marches against gun violence were held on March 24, 2018. They took place throughout the country and around the world.

SCHOOL SHOOTINGS

Since the 1970s, there have been hundreds of school shootings in the United States. They've happened in small towns and big cities. One of the most deadly was in 1999 in Littleton, Colorado. Two troubled teens shot and killed 13 people at Columbine High School, where they were students.

The Columbine shooters were young white men, as are most people who carry out mass shootings. They got their guns from older friends.

The attack shocked the country. At the time, it was the deadliest school shooting in U.S. history. Yet the government did little to prevent future mass shootings. Dozens more took place after the Columbine **massacre**.

This is a memorial to the 12 students and 1 teacher killed during the mass shooting at Columbine.

Although school shootings occur worldwide, most happen in the United States. Why? Experts think one of the main reasons is that guns are more widely available in this country than almost anywhere else. And there are few laws **regulating** them.

In 2007, a mentally ill college student opened fire at Virginia Tech, a university in Blacksburg, Virginia. The shooter killed 32 people and injured 23 others. Virginia Tech's **tragedy** became the deadliest school shooting in American history.

This is the campus of Virginia Tech where the shooting took place. Experts have different theories about why some people behave in such violent ways.

Then five years later, another disturbed young man in Newtown, Connecticut, killed 27 people at Sandy Hook Elementary School. "The majority of those who died today were children—beautiful little kids," said President Barack Obama after the shooting. "They had their entire lives ahead of them."

President Barack Obama

A father holds a photo of his young son, Daniel, who was killed at Sandy Hook Elementary School.

Americans were **outraged** over the Sandy Hook shooting. President Obama **proposed** new gun laws. The laws included **background checks** and banning certain guns, such as assault weapons. These weapons are most commonly used to carry out mass shootings. But the new gun laws did not pass. Why?

Guns kill 8 children per day in our nation. And, each year, around 36,000 Americans die from gun violence. However, there is a powerful group that believes most Americans should be able to own guns, even the deadliest kinds. This group has many supporters and a lot of influence on the government.

People can buy and sell guns at gun shows, like this one in Oklahoma.

In response to the shootings, about 95 percent of U.S. schools hold active shooter drills. This is when students and teachers practice hiding from an imaginary gunman

In February 2018, after the killing of 17 people at the Parkland, Florida, high school, the student survivors sprang into action. Cameron Kasky, a high school junior, said, "I had to skip the healing process and jump right into the fight."

A few days after the Parkland shooting, students took part in a "lie-in," where they pretended to be victims of gun violence.

Kasky and others started a group called #NeverAgain. The student activists demanded that lawmakers do something to stop gun violence in American schools. "I just want people to understand . . . that doing nothing will lead to nothing," said Kasky. A month after the shooting, they planned the March for Our Lives.

THE MARCH

Cameron Kasky, Emma González, David Hogg, and other student survivors led the march. The main goal of the protest was to push for new gun laws. The students wanted background checks on all gun sales and a ban on assault weapons.

Student organizers and survivors Emma González, David Hogg, Cameron Kasky, and Alex Wind

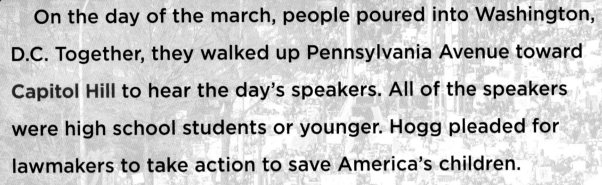

On the day of the march, people poured into Washington, D.C. Together, they walked up Pennsylvania Avenue toward Capitol Hill to hear the day's speakers. All of the speakers were high school students or younger. Hogg pleaded for lawmakers to take action to save America's children.

Before the march, the students raised more than $3 million and gave half to victims' families.

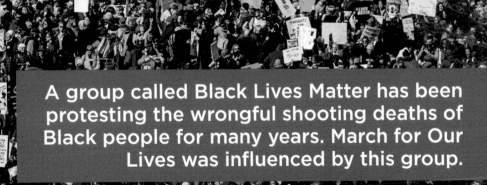

A group called Black Lives Matter has been protesting the wrongful shooting deaths of Black people for many years. March for Our Lives was influenced by this group.

Famous actors and singers also took part in the march. Singer Jennifer Hudson said she was "proud to stand with these brave students." Pop star Ariana Grande performed for the protesters. After singing her song "Be Alright," Grande said, "Thank you so much for fighting for change."

Ariana Grande performing at the March for Our Lives rally

The marchers sang along to the songs. They held homemade signs and posters covered with their own messages. "Protect kids, not guns!" they chanted in one loud voice.

NEVER AGAIN

Florida passed stricter gun laws in 2018. The laws raised the **minimum** age for buying guns to 21. "To the students of Marjory Stoneman Douglas High School, you made your voices heard. You didn't let up, and you fought until there was change," said Florida's governor after signing the new law.

However, Kasky and the other student activists know there is more work to do to stop gun-related deaths. But he's proud that the movement he helped create "has become a force that could change our country."

Since the Parkland shooting, 13 states have passed new gun laws. But few **federal** laws have been passed.

TIMELINE

1999   **April 20**
Mass shooting at Columbine High School in Littleton, Colorado, leaves 13 people dead.

2007   **April 16**
Mass shooting at Virginia Tech in Blacksburg, Virginia, leaves 32 people dead.

2012   **December 14**
Mass shooting at Sandy Hook Elementary School in Newtown, Connecticut, leaves 27 people dead, mostly young children.

2018   **February 14**
Mass shooting at Marjory Stoneman Douglas High School in Parkland, Florida, leaves 17 dead.

March 24
March for Our Lives takes place in Washington, D.C., and in other cities throughout the country and world.

March
Florida passes stricter gun laws.

GLOSSARY

activists (AK-tuh-vists) people who join together to fight for a cause

background checks (BAK-ground CHEKS) processes in which people are checked to make sure they are who they say they are and to see, for example, if they are criminals

Capitol Hill (KAP-ih-tuhl HIL) a small hill in Washington, D.C., where a building that serves as the center of government stands

federal (FED-ur-uhl) having to do with the national government

massacre (MAS-uh-kur) the killing of a large number of people

minimum (MIN-uh-muhm) the lowest amount or youngest age

outraged (OUT-rayjd) angered and shocked

proposed (pruh-POHZD) offered or suggested for acceptance or action

protest (PROH-test) an organized public gathering to influence or change something

regulating (REG-yuh-late-ing) controlling or supervising

tragedy (TRAJ-ih-dee) a sad and terrible event

victims (VIK-tuhmz) people who are hurt, injured, or killed by a person or event

violence (VYE-uh-luhns) behavior intended to hurt or kill someone

23

FIND OUT MORE

Books

Henderson, Leah. *Together We March: 25 Protest Movements That Marched into History*. New York: Atheneum Books, 2021.

Hudson, Wade, and Cheryl Willis Hudson, eds. *We Rise, We Resist, We Raise Our Voices*. New York: Crown Books for Young Readers, 2018.

Kluger, Jeffrey. *Raise Your Voice: 12 Protests That Shaped America*. New York: Philomel Books, 2020.

Websites

Giffords Law Center—Gun Violence Statistics
https://lawcenter.giffords.org/facts/gun-violence-statistics

March for Our Lives
https://marchforourlives.com

Sandy Hook Promise—16 Facts about Gun Violence and School Shootings
https://www.sandyhookpromise.org/gun-violence/16-facts-about-gun-violence-and-school-shootings

INDEX

ABOUT THE AUTHOR

Joyce Markovics is a writer and history buff. She loves learning about people and telling their stories. This book is dedicated to all the people who march for a more just future.